AGILITY TRAINING FOR DOGS

A BEGINNER'S STEP-BY-STEP GUIDE

JUAN'RI STRAUSS & MARGARET FRIEND

Table of Contents

Introduction

What do dogs need? As a dog owner, you'll probably name the necessities like food, water, and shelter. But of course, they also need stimulation. Most people provide their dogs with physical stimulation by going on walks or playing games like fetch or tug-of-war. But some forget that mental stimulation is essential to a dog's development. It helps keep a dog's mind active, curb boredom, and prevent destructive behavior from surfacing. And usually, dog owners would give their dogs mental interactive games or puzzles to feed their mental appetite. But what if you can combine both psychological and physical stimulation?

Agility training is the perfect way to achieve just that! Typically seen as another dog sport, owners teach their dogs to navigate various obstacles like jumps, hoops, or even seesaws. It's an excellent way to engage a dog's mind by allowing it to figure out how each obstacle works. At the same time, it helps burn excess energy and assists in obedience, making it the perfect training practice, especially for high-energy dogs. And the fun part is that you can learn how to train your dog to do agility courses by yourself. Get ready, and let us teach you the basics you need to know to get started.

Chapter 1:

What You Need to Know Before

You Start

While jumping head first into a new venture with your dog is fun, you must know a few things before starting. As you go through these essential tips and tricks, you'll get a sense of what agility training truly entails. Doing this will help you better prepare for this new adventure on which you and your canine friend will embark. So, without further ado, let's get to it.

What is Agility Training?

In 1978 organizers of the United Kingdom's Crufts Dog Show wanted an entertaining act between existing segments. John Varley worked with Peter Meanwell to create the first dog agility course. It looked similar to horse jumping courses and marked the beginning of the dog agility sport we know today.

But, it's quickly becoming more than just a competing sport because dog owners are more attentive to their dogs' mental and physical needs than ever before. These canine companions that live with us in our homes don't necessarily get the stimulation they need. Dog owners have to get creative. So, in comes dog agility for fun.

These agility activities include an array of jumping, balancing, weaving, and crawling. It activates your dog's body and mind while teaching it obedience and strengthening the bond you share. The type of obstacles include:

- The Dog Walk
- The A-Frame
- The Seesaw
- Open Tunnels
- Closed Tunnels
- The Bar Jump
- The Tire Jump
- Weave Poles
- The Table

These are fun for both dog and owner and an exceptionally stimulating pass-time activity for you both!

Where to Find Obstacles

Okay, now you may be intrigued by agility dog training but don't know where to get to the obstacles. Well, you have one of three choices:

- Look for a dog club near you that has agility obstacles and lessons and join them,

- Buy agility equipment online and train at home, or

- Make your own agility obstacles from storebought items.

If you want hands-on guidance on agility training, it's a good idea to consult trainers at your local dog club. But, if you're going to figure it out yourself, you can choose whether you want to buy or make agility equipment. In the end, the choice is up to you.

Special Considerations

Unfortunately, no matter how much you want to do agility training with your dog, some dogs can't. To know whether your dog can or can't partake in these fun activities, consider the following:

- **Is your dog a puppy?** A puppy's bones and joints aren't fully developed until 18-24 months old. Excess exercise, especially jumping or impact activities, can negatively influence bone and joint development. If you have a puppy, you shouldn't start with the jumping agility courses as it may harm your pup's growth.

- **Do you have a senior dog?** Some old dogs' bones and joints start to deteriorate, and impact exercises can worsen the condition. If you have a senior dog, ask your vet what agility exercises your dog can do first.

- **Does your dog have joint or bone issues?** Again, impact activities are strenuous on joints and bones. If, for instance, your dog has hip dysplasia, your dog might not be eligible for jumping agility. And if you're unsure, consult your vet to get the go-ahead.

- **How is your dog's overall health?** If your dog isn't 100% healthy, it may not be a good idea to do agility exercises. For example, excess activity can cause difficulty breathing if your dog has respiratory issues. Consider your dog's overall health before starting agility exercises.

You know your dog the best, so evaluate which agility activities it can do and which not. That way, you provide a safe, fun, and stimulating exercise you both can enjoy.

Dog Traits to Consider

While there are physical considerations, it's also a good idea to think about your dog's traits. That's because not all dogs are fit to do agility training. It depends on their temperament, reactivity, pack drive, prey drive, and breed. For example, if you have a skittish, aggressive dog, it might not fare well with agility training. At the same time, if your dog isn't energetic, it might prefer to laze around instead of navigating through obstacles. So, let's consider the different traits in more detail.

Temperament

Your dog's temperament is how it reacts to other people and dogs and can be inherited or created through environmental factors. Your dog's character could be assertive, aggressive, neutral, or passive. Of course, the best traits for agility would be a dog that is outgoing, energetic, and lacking aggression. That's because confidence and energy would encourage your dog to explore and navigate new obstacles. But, if it is aggressive, it might get triggered on the course and lash out at other people or dogs nearby. You'd want your dog to be assertive or neutral to adapt to agility exercises.

Assertive/ Aggressive Temperaments

An assertive dog is confident and curious, always looking to do things the way it prefers, and won't shy away from a challenge or stressful situation. These dogs can come across as fearless and fierce protectors and can even become aggressive if you don't have a handle on their behaviors.

Assertive dogs have the following characteristics:

- They are possessive

- They are territorial

- They will push boundaries

- They play tug a lot and won't give up until they win

- Their play fighting often turns into a real fight

- They will pull on the lead when you go for a walk

- They're less likely to respond to verbal cues when they're focussed on something else

- They are bold and often unafraid

- They play roughly with their toys, often destroying them in the process

- They have a good prey drive

- They're confident

Luckily, it doesn't mean that your assertive dog will become aggressive. You must put extra effort into obedience training and getting rid of excess energy. And when you have an assertive dog, it might learn to navigate the obstacles quicker.

Neutral Temperaments

Dogs with neutral temperaments are calm and confident, all in one package. It is easier to train neutral dogs because they respect boundaries, especially when using positive reinforcement. These dogs can walk into an unfamiliar situation without feeling anxious. Still, they would walk away or be more passive in the face of trouble.

Neutral dogs have the following characteristics:

- They prefer to play fetch instead of tug-of-war

- They have a decent prey drive but would choose to befriend someone instead

- They're more gentle with their toys, not destroying them as quick as assertive dogs

- They handle stress well and can cope during tense situations

- On walks, they would check in with you instead of needlessly pulling on the leash

- They love playing with other dogs, and the play sessions never turn aggressive

- They choose to avoid conflict instead of encouraging it

- They are great sharers and won't get possessive with their food or toys

- They usually won't become destructive when they're bored

These dogs are exceptionally good at self-soothing their nerves and navigating agility obstacles. They also know how to respect boundaries but still have enough courage to face unfamiliar environments. The ideal temperament for agility is a neutral one.

Passive Temperaments

Passive dogs are pretty timid and lack confidence in their everyday lives. They would skeptically enter unfamiliar environments and tread carefully in any situation. Things like loud noises tend to scare them, and they're known to struggle with anxiety. They don't know how to cope in stressful situations and find it difficult to soothe their nerves.

- Passive dogs have the following characteristics:

- They won't interact with other dogs or people

- They prefer to stick to your side or keep to themselves in a corner

- They don't typically like to play with toys, but if they do, they don't damage them at all

- They can be severely anxious and suffer from conditions like separation anxiety

- It's a challenge to get a suitable training method to use with them (usually, positive reinforcement is the best way to go, but it takes lots of love, patience, and understanding)

- They have little to no prey drive

- They are apprehensive most of the time, especially when encountering something new

These dogs can be challenging to train because they don't have the confidence to go out and try something new. Even if you speak too loud at them, they might get frightened and freeze up instead of performing the cue. If you have a passive dog, it might struggle with agility training. Luckily, you can work on your dog's confidence and make agility training a fun and safe experience.

If you think your dog has undesirable agility traits but you want to take part in those activities, you could speak to a trainer. Dogs can unlearn some behaviors (primarily taught behaviors) through consistent positive training, and they could learn to love agility.

Reactivity

Your dog reacts a certain way to environmental factors, like loud noises, random passers-by, or other animals approaching. This reactivity could manifest in a few different ways. It could startle easily, which could increase feelings of fear and anxiety, or it could handle unexpected stimuli. For example, your dog could bark, lunge, or growl at a trigger. Or it could be neutral toward it and go about its day like it typically would. And for a dog to adapt to the environment of agility, it mustn't be reactive. Otherwise, your dog could startle easily, get frightened, and create negative associations with agility.

It doesn't mean you won't excel in agility training if you have a reactive dog. It just means you'll have to put in extra effort to desensitize it toward triggers. Here's how you'll do it:

Find the trigger:

Figure out what triggers your dog. Is it loud noises or other dogs passing by your home? Does it bark excessively at cars, or is it fearful of people entering its personal space? Once you can pinpoint the trigger, you can start desensitizing your dog. That way, you teach your dog that it doesn't need to react to the stimulus and is safe.

Slow exposure to the stimulus at a distance:

Now that you know what triggers your dog's reactivity, you can expose it to the trigger and work on its reactivity. For example, if your dog is scared of loud noises, make sudden sounds in your house by throwing metal items on the floor or loudly shutting the cabinets. Then, throw a treat at your dog. This way, your dog will hear the sound, get the treat, and slowly create a positive association with loud noises.

On the other hand, if your dog is scared of other people, cars, or dogs, put it on a leash and have a treat bag ready. Then, go where your dog can see the trigger (people or cars), but be far enough away that your dog doesn't react. You can slowly decrease the distance between your dog and the trigger without responding to it. Then, if your dog seems relaxed, give it a treat. And when it looks at you, provide a reward. This way, your dog learns it doesn't have to fear triggers and can look up to you for guidance.

Reward calm reactions:

Giving a treat at the right time is essential. Know how your dog usually reacts and rewards the opposite calm behavior. For example, if your dog usually barks uncontrollably at something in the distance, give a treat when it stops barking. Soon, your dog will learn that there are more rewarding experiences by your side than worrying about what is in the distance.

Ignore reactive reactions:

When your dog reacts by barking or pulling on the leash, the worst thing you can do is scold it. For example, if your dog barks out of fear or to alert danger and yell at it to stop, it interprets your yelling as barking. This gives your dog the idea that it has something to fear because its owner also "barks." At the same time, if your dog lunges at something, don't scold it. Walk away in the other direction and reward your dog when it calms down.

Slowly get closer to the trigger:

Once your dog seems reliably calm at a certain distance, gradually increase the proximity to the stimulus. Then, continue to follow the tips mentioned above.

Be consistent with rewards:

Consistency is an essential aspect of dog training. The more you stick to your rules, reactions, and rewards, the quicker your dog will catch on to what you expect it to do.

Be calm:

Your dog can sense your emotions. If you're stressed or angry, your dog will feel it and go into an anxious state, especially if you take it out on your dog. Whenever you feel frustrated with your dog, take a deep breath and try to calm yourself.

These tips aren't only applicable to reactivity but many different dog training activities. When it comes to agility, you can use these to help your dog get used to new obstacles if it seems wary at first. It's a good skill for any dog owner to have.

Pack and Prey Drive

Your dog's level of pack and prey drive plays an integral part in its success in agility training. That's because its instincts will guide its navigation of the obstacles. It will also improve your dog's willingness to work as a team with you, the owner. But to understand this, we first need to look at what pack and prey drive are:

Pack drive is your dog's desire to be part of a group or pack. Its affinity to people and other pets usually dictates how well it fits into its environment. For example, a low pack drive means your dog doesn't necessarily want to be in a group and is more independent. On the other hand, a high pack drive could mean your dog gets anxious whenever it's alone and can become overly clingy. Ideally, you'd want your dog to be somewhere in between to fit into the world of agility.

A good pack drive means that your dog will respect rules and boundaries and can follow instructions. This is essential in agility because you'll be the one guiding your dog through the course. And if your dog can't follow pack instructions or is too clingy and won't move away from you, it will make agility more challenging.

Prey drive is your dog's instinct to find, chase, and catch prey. But, how the prey drive manifests differs from dog to dog. For example, a border collie stalks and herds prey to a specific destination. On the other hand, beagles have exceptional scenting abilities, making them perfect for tracking. Your dog's eagerness to find, chase, and catch prey will undoubtedly make agility training easier and more fun. That's because you tap into and use your dog's natural abilities to teach it how to navigate the obstacles.

A good prey drive is helpful to train agility initially because your dog will follow a toy or treat. You can use this ability to smell (track), chase (follow), and catch (eat) the prey (treat or toy). Unfortunately, dogs are born with a high or low prey drive; their genetics determines it. Some dogs like Siberian Huskies, Jack Russels, and Border Collies have naturally high prey drives. On the other hand, some dogs have naturally low prey drives, like Cavelier King Charles Spaniels, Boxers, and French Bulldogs. As you can see, pack and prey drives play a massive role in agility compatibility.

However, it doesn't mean that dogs with low prey drives can't do agility. With enough training and patience, they can excel just as well as any other breed.

Breeds

You might know that over the years, dogs were bred for specific purposes, like hunting, tracking, and protection work, to name a few. People managed it by breeding dogs with particular traits and creating the hundreds of dog breeds available today. That's why some dog breeds are more prone to like and excel in agility training than others. It's no secret that certain breeds do exceptionally well in these competitions, like:

- Border Collies
- Australian Shepherds
- Shetland Sheepdogs
- Golden Retrievers
- Jack Russel Terriers
- Cocker Spaniels
- Papillons
- Whippits
- Poodles

Although you know that some breeds perform better in agility activities, you might wonder why it plays such a massive role.

How Breed Traits Influence Its Agility Ability

Because dogs were bred for specific purposes, they have particular traits depending on the breed. Some characteristics are excellent for agility work, while others might not be as suitable.

Breed Categories and Eligibility

Seven main dog breed groups with different dog breeds bred to perform the same roles. All the breeds in a specific group have similar behavioral traits, temperaments, energy levels, and intelligence. These groups are:

- Herding breeds

- Hound breeds

- Non-Sporting breeds

- Sporting breeds

- Terrier breeds

- Toy breeds

- Working breeds

So, let's examine each breed group and whether they would be good agility dogs.

Herding Breeds

Dogs in the herding breed were initially bred to assist human shepherds in their tasks. These dogs had to round up animals (usually livestock), herd the animals to specific locations, and protect these animals from predators at night. They are naturally hard-working, intelligent, high-energy dogs, making them perfect for agility activities. That's why many Border Collies, Australian Shepherds, and German Shepherds compete in agility competitions.

Hound Breeds

Dogs in the hound group were bred initially to help hunters hunt warm-blooded quarries. These animals include squirrels, rabbits, ducks, and geese who lived in pits made of different materials like rocks or water holes. Because hound breeds rely on their scent and sight to help hunters, they have exceptional sniffing and seeking abilities. And because of their hunting abilities, they are intelligent, intuitive, and energetic to participate in agility competitions. Some hound breeds that typically excel in agility are Beagles and Greyhounds.

Non-Sporting Breeds

Dogs in the non-sporting group don't quite fit into the other six dog breed groups. Each different breed may have been bred for a specific purpose, but not one that can perfectly fit into the other groups. For instance, some of these dogs may have been bred to help people hunt, but what they hunt and their role in the hunting process may differ from the original hunting group. It depends on the individual dog's traits. And because of this group's wide variety of breeds, it isn't easy to pinpoint which will excel in agility.

For example, three Breeds under this group include the Dalmatian, French Bulldog, and Poodle. Both Dalmatians and Poodles are intelligent, learn quickly, are energetic, and do well in agility activities. On the other hand, French Bulldogs are less known for their athletic abilities. They won't necessarily make the best natural agility competitor. But again, it doesn't mean these dogs can't do agility. They just need a little more training than those with a natural affinity for navigating obstacles.

Sporting Breeds

Dogs in the sporting group were initially bred to help hunters track the game birds or waterfowl they'd shot. Because people used hunting rifles, they didn't need dogs to do the hunting anymore. They discovered, however, that they needed dogs to help track the birds or fowl after the hunters shot them. Because they didn't die on impact, the birds or fowl made some way into water or uphill, which would be difficult for the hunters to find. They were essentially a hunter's right-hand man (or canine in this case).

Because agility is a dog sport, the sporting breeds typically excel in these activities. Two breed examples are Cocker Spaniels and Golden Retrievers. They have exceptional prey and pack drives and easily navigate through different obstacles.

Terrier Breeds

Dogs in the Terrier group were originally bred to hunt and kill small animals like rats and badgers and protect their family's home. Each dog's purpose would differ depending on where the dog was located. For example, some would only need to keep rats out of the kitchen, while others had to stand watch at the front door.

Most terriers are stubborn and need a little more focus on obedience before they can excel in agility activities. But, once you get that underway, they have the energy, intellect, and willingness to navigate the obstacles. Two incredible examples are Scottish Terriers and Jack Russel Terriers.

Toy Breeds

Dogs in the toy group were initially bred as companions to people. Their tiny bodies make them easily transportable, often in carrier bags so that people can take their beloved companions anywhere. The only job these dogs have is to keep their human's company, providing love and affection along the way. These dogs are the perfect dogs for apartment living or people who don't have a lot of space at home.

Although these dogs are mostly companion animals, they can have incredible agility abilities. For example, they are usually quite energetic, curious, and eager to please their owners. Toy breed dogs like the Chihuahua, Maltese, and Pomeranian are excellent at navigating agility obstacles. But, like the non-sporting breeds, it will depend from dog to dog and their traits.

Working Breeds

The working breeds were initially grouped with the sporting breeds but got their own group because they performed more specific jobs. Today, these breeds make excellent service animals, allowing emergency personnel to make their jobs easier. These dogs would usually help in tasks like pulling a sled, assisting rescue missions, protecting people, or guarding flocks, like police or drug-sniffing dogs.

As suggested in the name, working breed dogs love to work. When they have a goal and purpose, they thrive using their intelligence and drive to meet those goals. And agility obstacles are just another form of work for these dogs. Some of the working breeds that do well in agility are Alaskan Malamutes and Rottweilers, no matter how unexpected it may seem.

However, it doesn't mean that other dogs won't excel. Almost all breeds can do agility training, including mixed breeds, as long as you put in enough effort and if your dog shows interest in the activities.

Of course, the question comes in whether your dog's breed is allowed to participate in agility competitions. Well, almost all dog breeds can participate in a variety of classes. For example, breed sizes compete against each other. In that case, a Chihuahua won't be measured against a Border Collie. It just won't be fair. If you want to compete with your dog, look at the guidelines:

- The American Kennel Club,

- The Australian National Kennel Council, or the

- Kennel Club UK (depending on where you plan to compete).

We'll discuss these three associations in more detail later in the ebook. For now, you can check their websites and familiarise yourself with the rules and regulations of agility competitions or trials.

Cues and Rewards

The basis of any training is to have the right cue and reward system. The cue is the word you'll say to prompt a specific reaction in your dog. For example, "jump" means jump over whatever is in its line of sight. At the same time, the reward is a tasty treat you'll give your dog for a job well done. For instance, if your dog successfully did the action you wanted it to do, give a treat. That way, you use positive reinforcement to teach your dog how the agility activities work and encourage your dog to perform those activities reliably. But how exactly does it work?

Well, a cue is a unique word for a specific activity. You'll use one word or phrase per action and nothing else. Here are the typical cues people use in agility and their meaning:

- Over: Whenever your dog needs to walk over something, like the dog walk, A-frame, or seesaw.

- Under: When your dog needs to crawl or walk underneath something over its head, like the bed.

- Through: This is a bit different than "under." In this case, your dog needs to go through something that will enclose its body, like the open and closed tunnels.

- Up: You'll say this whenever your dog has to make a jumping motion. You'll use it with any of the jumps.

- Heel: To have your dog walk by your side. This is one of two commands you'll use to teach your dog the weaving poles. Usually, your dog should be on your left-hand side when you say the heel command.

- In: The second command you'll use with the weaving poles is to get your dog to move away from you when it's in a heel position.

You'll use those most common cues along with your dog's reward of choice. This combination is essential to help your dog understand how to do each agility activity. The more you practice using the step-by-step guidelines in chapter two, the less you'll have to use rewards and only rely on commands. Soon, you can stand in the middle of the obstacles and point at an obstacle while saying a cue, and your dog will be able to do it flawlessly. But remember that this takes practice, patience, and lots of praise.

Chapter 2:

Step-by-Step Agility Training Guide

It's time to learn how to teach your dog to do the different agility activities. These include obstacles, tunnels, jumps, weave poles, and the table. So, get your agility items ready, have a handful of treats available, and get your dog. Then, with each activity, you'll start slowly. Your dog doesn't understand these activities yet, so you must teach them. The only way to do that is to show it step-by-step and reward each good action. Never get frustrated with your dog or punish it for not doing what you've asked. Your dog doesn't do what you want because it doesn't understand the cue. Be patient. If your dog struggles, take a break and start from scratch.

Heel

While the "heel" cue isn't an agility activity, it forms part of the foundation of agility work. For a dog to be on heel means walking on the owner's left-hand side. Whenever you say "heel," your dog is supposed to go to your left-hand side and match your pace and direction. It's a bit tricky initially, but you can easily teach it to your dog before starting any other agility work. Here's how you'll do it:

1. Put your dog's collar on, attach the leash, and prepare a treat bag.

2. Stand next to your sitting dog, both facing in the same direction. Your dog should be on your left-hand side, also known as the heel position.

3. Take a treat with your left hand, and hold it against your dog's nose, but don't let it eat the treat yet.

4. Then, take one step forward while saying the cue "heel." Your dog should follow the treat in your hand and, subsequently, you.

5. Repeat steps 2-4 until your dog reliably follows you when you step forward.

6. Then, step forward without a treat this time, but still say heel. Your dog should be conditioned by now to follow you when you say heel.

7. The better your dog gets, the more steps you can take. The idea is that your dog walks on your left, not only to take a few steps. While you walk, say the cue "heel" a few times, so your dog learns what it means to walk by your side.

8. If your dog struggles, you can lure it into place with a treat. Eventually, you can phase out the treats and only rely on your cue to get your dog into position.

9. As you practice this at home, be consistent. Don't let your dog take the treat if it didn't walk by your side. Instead, try luring it into place again, then give the reward. The more you do this, the quicker your dog will come to your side, no matter where it is or how distracted it may be.

Contact Obstacles

There are three obstacles you can start teaching your dog to maneuver. These are the dog walk, seesaw, and A-frame, and you'll use the command "over" with these obstacles. But, if you have a puppy, you shouldn't do the A-frame just yet. That's because dogs typically give a small jump at the end of the obstacle, which can damage your puppy's joints. Don't worry, though. You can still do the dog walk and seesaw safely with your pup.

The Dog Walk

The dog walk is probably the biggest obstacle on any agility course. It consists of three planks mounted together. The middle plank is horizontal with the ground, while the two at the ends form the uphill (where your dog will climb onto the obstacle) and downhill (where your dog will climb off). Regarding competition-grade guidelines, there will be yellow contact strips, which is where your dog's paws should touch. This way, it prevents your dog from jumping while using this obstacle or running over it too fast. Here's how you'll teach your dog to do the dog walk:

1. Put on your dog's collar and leash and have a treat bag ready.

2. Stand with your dog in heel position in front of the dog walk. The idea is that your dog is directly in front of the dog walk so it can walk in a straight line onto the structure. And it would be best if you were on your dog's right side (your dog on your left).

3. Hold the leash in your left hand, ensuring your dog can't trip over it (the easiest way to do this is to bundle it up in your hand and hold it above your dog's back). At the same time, don't tighten the leash. When a leash is tight around your dog's neck, it thinks it's doing something wrong.

4. Hold a treat in your right hand, say the cue "over," and lure your dog to walk onto the dog walk.

5. Most dogs don't have spatial development yet, so they don't know where to put their feet on such a thin surface. Ensure you're close enough to your dog to prevent it from falling off.

6. Some dogs are a bit scared initially, so that they might need extra help. If this is your dog, hold its body with your left hand (the one holding the leash), lure it with a treat in your right hand, and give a gentle push on the body with the left hand.

7. Never pull your dog with the leash, as it can cause a negative association and increase anxiety around the obstacle. The more fun it is, the more your dog will want to do it.

8. Practice these steps a few times, and once your dog gets the hang of things, you can let it do the activity by itself. For example, you'll walk to the ramp with your dog on a leash. And without using a treat, you say your cue "over" and let your dog do the activity by itself. Remember, even though you don't use treats, praise your dog verbally for a job well done.

The Seesaw

The seesaw, also known as a teeter, is one plank on a central pivot point structure. The idea is that your dog walks onto the plank, calmly continues as the center of mass pivots, and continues walking on the entire length as the plank hits the ground. While it sounds easy, it can be tricky because dogs usually get a fright the first time the plank hits the ground after it pivots. Some dogs also jump off the seesaw before it hits the ground, which shouldn't happen if you want to go into agility competitions. But, because these are the basic guidelines, let's first learn how to get our dogs comfortable maneuvering the teeter. Here's how you'll do it:

1. Put on your dog's collar and leash and have a treat bag ready.

2. Put a pillow (or something else) under the seesaw end to soften the sound it hits the ground. That way, you prevent your dog from getting scared by the noise and ensure a positive association with the obstacle. Once you've done the exercise with the pillow a few times, you can take it away and start the steps from scratch.

3. Stand with your dog in heel position in front of the seesaw. Your dog should be directly in front of the seesaw so it can walk in a straight line onto the structure. And it would be best if you were on your dog's right side (your dog on your left).

4. Hold the leash in your left hand, ensuring your dog can't trip over it (The easiest way to do this is to bundle it up in your hand and hold it above your dog's back). At the same time, don't tighten the leash. When a leash is tight around your dog's neck, it thinks it's doing something wrong.

5. Hold a treat in your right hand, say the cue "over," and lure your dog to walk onto the seesaw.

6. Give your dog the treat when the plank starts to move at the pivot point. That's because it might get a fright from the movement, so that the treat will act as extra encouragement.

7. Once your dog gets to the end of the seesaw, give another treat.

8. Most dogs don't have spatial development yet, so they don't know where to put their feet on such a thin surface. Ensure you're close enough to your dog to prevent it from falling off.

9. Some dogs are a bit scared initially, so that they might need extra help. If this is your dog, hold its body with your left hand (the one holding the leash), lure it with a treat in your right hand, and give a gentle push on the body with the left hand.

10. Never pull your dog with the leash, as it can cause a negative association and increase anxiety around the obstacle. The more fun it is, the more your dog will want to do it.

Practice these steps a few times, and once your dog gets the hang of things, you can let it do the activity by itself. For example, you'll walk to the teeter with your dog on a leash. And without using a treat, you say your cue "over" and let your dog do the activity by itself. Remember, even though you don't use treats, praise your dog verbally for a job well done.

The A-Frame

The A-frame is two planks propped at an angle to form a triangle or A-shape. It also has smaller horizontal planks sprayed on the surface to give your dog a grip when it climbs over the frame. The part of each plank that touches the ground has a different color marking, usually 42 inches, which is touch zones. It means your dog should touch the uphill touch zone when it climbs onto the A-frame and the downhill touch zone when it gets off. That prevents your dog from jumping or sprinting on the obstacle. Here's how to teach your dog to do the A-frame:

1. Put on your dog's collar and leash and have a treat bag ready.
2. Stand with your dog in heel position in front of the A-frame. The idea is that your dog is directly in front of the A-frame so it can walk in a straight line onto the structure. And it would be best if you were on your dog's right side (your dog on your left).
3. Hold the leash in your left hand, ensuring your dog can't trip over it (The easiest way to do this is to bundle it up in your hand and hold it above your dog's back. At the same time, don't tighten the leash. When a leash is tight around your dog's neck, it thinks it's doing something wrong.
4. Hold a treat in your right hand, say the cue "over," and lure your dog to walk onto the A-frame.
5. Most dogs will stop at the top of the frame. If that happens with yours, continue luring it with a treat to come down.
6. Some dogs are a bit scared initially, so that they might need extra help. If this is your dog, hold its body with your left hand (the one holding the leash), lure it with a treat in your

right hand, and give a gentle push on the body with the left hand.

7. Never pull your dog with the leash, as it can cause a negative association and increase anxiety around the obstacle. The more fun it is, the more your dog will want to do it.

Practice these steps a few times, and once your dog gets the hang of things, you can let it do the activity by itself. For example, you'll walk to the frame with your dog on a leash. And without using a treat, you say your cue "over" and let your dog do the activity by itself. Remember, even though you don't use treats, praise your dog verbally for a job well done.

Tunnels

Tunnels are long, round structures of various materials that are straight or bent through which your dog should maneuver. Typically, you'll start with a shorter, straight tunnel to teach your dog how to go through it while you use the cue "through." The better your dog gets with the action, the more you can ramp up the level of challenge. You'll start with short, straight, open tunnels, then longer, bent, open tunnels, and finally move on to the closed tunnels.

Open Tunnels

Open tunnels refer to tunnels that have an open round structure. These can be long or short, straight, or bent. If the tunnel is straight, you can see from one end to the other as you look through it. Here's how to teach your dog to walk through an open tunnel:

1. Start with a short open tunnel and let your dog sit in front of it. It's easiest if your dog knows how to do a sit stay so that it stays in place while you get into position.

2. You'll move to the other end of the tunnel with a treat in your hand.

3. Look at your dog through the tunnel, show it the treat, and call it to come to you.

4. Repeat steps 1-3 a few times until your dog reliably goes through the tunnel.

5. Then, let your dog stand in front of the tunnel, on your left-hand side, and say the word "through."

6. Give a treat and verbal praise when your dog comes out at the other end.

7. If your dog doesn't want to go through the tunnel while you're by their side, get someone to help you. Let the other person stand at the other end of the tunnel like you initially did with a treat in their hand. Then, follow steps 5 and 6 while your friend shows your dog the treat.

The more you practice this, the quicker your dog will move through the open tunnel, and the less you will need treats to get the job done. Then, only when your dog reliably goes through the open tunnel can you start training it to go through closed ones.

Closed Tunnels

Closed tunnels have a sturdy barrel-like entrance like an open tunnel, and they can be long or short, straight or bent. But they have one fundamental difference from open tunnels: it has a material chute tunnel through which your dog must go. If you straighten the tunnel, you can't see from one end to the other because the material chute is collapsed. And while the action is the same as the open tunnel, your dog might be confused with this one. Here's how to teach your dog to go through it:

1. Start with a short, straight, closed tunnel and let your dog sit in front of it. It's easiest if your dog knows how to do a "sit-stay" to stay in place while you get into position.

2. You'll move to the other end of the tunnel with a treat in your hand.

3. Lift the material chute so your dog can see you through the tunnel and the treat.

4. Call your dog to you and give it a treat once it passes through.

5. Repeat steps 1-4 until your dog reliably goes through the tunnel.

6. Slowly increase the difficulty level by lowering the material chute little by little and following steps 1-4. Eventually, you won't hold the tube, and your dog will go through the tunnel.

7. Then, let your dog stand in front of the tunnel, on your left-hand side, and say the word "through."

8. Give a treat and verbal praise when your dog comes out at the other end.

9. If your dog doesn't want to go through the tunnel while you're by their side, get someone to help you. Let the other person stand at the other end of the tunnel like you initially did with a treat in their hand. Then, follow steps 7 and 8 while your friend shows your dog the treat.

The more you practice this, the quicker your dog will move through the open tunnel, and the less you will need treats to get the job done. And once your dog gets the hang of it, you can bend the tunnel in different directions for your dog to navigate through.

Jumps

Most dogs love jump agility, so it's an excellent way to eliminate your dog's excess energy and provide physical stimulation. These jumps refer to any agility activity where your dog has to make a jumping motion, including bar and tire jumps. And the cue you'll use is the word "up." Of course, you can say "jump" if you want to. If you stick to the same command every time, you're good to go. But remember that jumps might not be the best activity for your health if you have a puppy, an elderly dog, or one with health issues.

The Bar Jump

The bar jump is an adjustable horizontal pole held up by two structures (usually a vertical pole and a stand on each end) and looks like an H. You can adjust the bar depending on your dog's size and advancement level, and the idea is that your dog runs up to the bar and jumps once you say "up." Unfortunately, some dogs can be scared of the bar first, so you must start easy and work your way up to a proper jump. Here's how to do it:

1. Set the bar on the ground first for your dog to walk over. Starting with a low bar will help your dog get used to the activity.

2. Put on your dog's collar and leash and prepare a treat bag.

3. Let your dog stand in line with the bar jump on your left side so it can move straight to the jump.

4. Walk with your dog toward the jump in a heel position. Then say the word "up" when your dog should jump.

5. Give your dog a treat for a successful attempt.

6. Repeat steps 1-5 until your dog reliably does what you ask. Slowly increase the difficulty level by raising the bar an inch at a time.

7. As you raise the bar height, running with your dog to the jump might be easier than walking. Then, repeat steps 4-5 each time you raise the bar. That way, your dog gets leverage and can make a higher jump.

8. Reward your dog for a job well done.

Eventually, all you have to do is stand at a distance, point at a jump, and say the word "up." That's because your dog will know what the cue means and form positive, fun associations with the activity that it will want to do what you command.

The Tire Jump

The tire jump is a tire suspended in the air with a frame-like structure through which your dog should jump. These are different heights and sizes, depending on your dog's breed, and your dog must know the basic bar jump before you can attempt this activity. But, if you want to get started with this earlier, you can get a hula hoop and get your dog used to jumping through a circular structure. This way, you work your dog's way up to the tire jump. Here's how to teach your dog the tire jump:

Using the Hula Hoop

You can buy any hula hoop to get your dog used to jumping through a circular object. Here's how to teach your dog to do it:

1. Set the edge hula hoop on the ground first to form a circle where your dog should walk. Starting that low will help your dog get used to the activity. You can decide whether you want a friend to hold the hoop in place, or you can fasten it somehow.

2. Put on your dog's collar and leash and prepare a treat bag.

3. Let your dog stand in line with the hula hoop on your left side so it can move straight to the jump.

4. Walk with your dog toward the hoop in a heel position. Then say the word "up" when your dog should jump.

5. Give your dog a treat for a successful attempt.

6. Repeat steps 1-5 until your dog reliably does what you ask. Slowly increase the difficulty level by raising the hoop an inch at a time.

7. As you raise the hula hoop height, running with your dog might be easier than walking. Then, repeat steps 4-5 each time you increase the hoop height. That way, your dog gets leverage and can make a higher jump.

8. Reward your dog for a job well done.

Once your dog is comfortable jumping through the hoop at a raised height, you can let it jump through the tire instead.

How to Teach the Tire Jump

The tire jump is the same concept as the bar jump. The only difference is that it is a tire suspended in the air. Here's how to get your dog to do it:

1. Put on your dog's collar and leash and prepare a treat bag.

2. Let your dog stand in line with the tire jump on your left side so it can move straight to the jump.

3. Run with your dog toward the jump in a heel position. Then say the word "up" when your dog should jump.

4. Give your dog a treat for a successful attempt.

5. Repeat steps 1-4 until your dog reliably does what you ask, and continue to reward your dog for a job well done.

6. If your dog doesn't want to jump, it might be a good idea to start with the hula hoop exercise until your dog grasps the concept.

Eventually, all you have to do is stand at a distance, point at a jump, and say the word "up." That's because your dog will know what the cue means and form positive, fun associations with the activity that it will want to do what you command.

Weave Poles

Weave poles are usually 6 or 12 horizontal poles in a straight line through which your dog should weave. The two commands you'll use are "in" and "heel." Some people prefer to use "in" and "out," but if you already teach your dog to walk on heel and be by your left side when you say "heel," it's easier to work that cue into this activity. Then, when you're ready, here's how to teach your dog to move through the weaving poles:

1. Put on your dog's collar and leash and have treats ready.

2. Let your dog stand on your left-hand side and in line with the poles. The idea is that your dog can walk straight to the bars and start the activity.

3. Hold the leash above your dog's body in your left hand to ensure it doesn't dangle in front of its face or get stuck on the poles. The easiest way is to hold the leash in a bundle above your dog's body.

4. Hold a treat in your right hand to lure your dog through the poles. Your dog's first move is "in," meaning that the first pole should be on your left side, and your dog should move away from you for the first weave.

5. With the treat against your dog's nose, let your dog move away from you while you say "in."

6. Then, the second pole should be between you and your dog. Lure your dog back to you with the treat while saying "heal."

7. You'll continue to lure your dog in a weaving motion through the poles, using the cues "in" (when your dog moves away from you into the weave) and "heel" (when your dog moves back toward your side, completing the weave).

The more you practice this, your dog will associate the poles with the "in" and "heal" commands. Eventually, you can pick up the pace, and your dog will do the weaving bars without treats or continuous cues. But first, work on teaching your dog how the activity works.

The Table

The table is a table-like structure with mesh instead of a countertop; its height depends on your dog's size. Small dog breeds will have a lower table than large dog breeds. The idea is for your dog to crawl underneath the table from one end to the other. Some dogs love it and catch on quickly, but others are wary about the structure above their bodies. It's a good idea to start with a high enough structure for your dog to walk through, then slowly lower it until it is in a crawling position. Here's how to teach your dog to crawl under the table:

1. Put on your dog's leash and collar while having treats ready.

2. Start with the table at a height your dog can freely walk under without its back touching the tip.

3. Let your dog sit and stay in front of the table while you get into position.

4. You'll move to the other end of the table with a treat in your hand.

5. Look at your dog underneath the table, show it the treat, and call it to come to you.

6. Repeat steps 1-3 a few times until your dog reliably walks under the table to get to you and the treat.

7. Then, let your dog stand in front of the table, on your left-hand side, and say the word "under." Your dog should move under the table. But if it doesn't, you can lure it with a treat. Do this by walking outside the table while the treat hand is in front of your dog's nose under the table.

8. Give a treat and verbal praise when your dog comes out at the other end.

9. If your dog doesn't want to go under the table while you're by their side, get someone to help you. Let the other person stand at the other end like you initially did with a treat in their hand. Then, follow steps 7 and 8 while your friend shows your dog the treat.

The more you practice this, the more your dog will easily walk under the table. Then, you can slowly lower the table to get your dog into a crawling position. Eventually, your dog will crawl under the table with only the cue, not the treats.

Chapter 3:

Agility Organizations

There are many dog-related organizations worldwide that set standards for dog ownership. It's a matter of forging good dog ownership and providing an informative platform for dog enthusiasts everywhere. It includes creating guidelines for dog health, breeding, exercise, training, etc. But what does this have to do with agility, you may ask? Well, agility is a dog sport where dogs can compete against one another for various titles. And like any sporting event, you need judges, competition guidelines, rules, and structure. Without them, anyone can create obstacles for dogs, which might not be safe for the canine body. Organizations like the American Kennel Club, The Australian National Kennel Council, and the Kennel Club in the UK step up to the plate.

The American Kennel Club (AKC)

"Founded in 1884, the not-for-profit AKC is the recognized and trusted expert in breed, health, and training information for all dogs. AKC actively advocates for responsible dog ownership and is dedicated to advancing dog sports" (American Kennel Club).

Agility Competition Regulations

The AKC gives access to agility competitions for dogs of all ages, sizes, and breeds (including mixed breeds). If you have a dog that loves to do agility, you'll get a suitable competition near you on their website. Of course, like any regulatory body, a few special requirements will make a dog eligible to compete in their category.

Eligibility Requirements

If you want to compete with your dog, look at the complete list of the AKC's agility regulations, which describe a dog's eligibility requirements. For example, some conditions are that your dog must:

- Be older than 15 months.

- Spayed or neutered.

- Not be in heat (if you have a female dog).

- Be registered at the AKC or acknowledged organization (see the list on the AKC website).

- Be of good health and sound mind.

- Not be blind, bandaged, or have any attached medical equipment to the body.

Breed Requirements

As you know, all dog breeds can participate in agility competitions. But that doesn't mean that your dog can compete in them all. That's because some clubs might choose to host breed-specific events. Your Cocker Spaniel won't be eligible if they have a German Shepherd agility event. It depends primarily on the exact competition you want to sign up for.

The Australian National Kennel Council (ANKC)

Founded in 1949, the ANKC is another non-profit organization with the following mission statement: "To promote excellence in breeding, showing, trialling, obedience and other canine-related activities and the ownership of temperamentally and physically sound pure bred dogs by responsible individuals across Australia. To promote responsible dog ownership and encourage State Member Bodies to put in place programs to that effect. To act as spokesperson on all canine-related activities on a National basis on behalf of State Member Bodies and to pledge assistance and support to the respective State Member Bodies" (The Australian National Kennel Council).

Agility Competition Regulations

Like the AKC, their Australian counterparts, the ANKC, also opens agility competitions for all sorts of dogs, no matter their breed. Your mixed-breed dog can compete, too, if you'd like. But again, some dogs might not be eligible to compete, so the ANKC has a few regulations regarding these competitions. Let's see what they are.

Eligibility Requirements

Each agility competition has its own set of agility requirements, depending on which category you sign up for. Look at the ANKC website and their specific competition requirements. But, some general eligibility requirements are that your dog must:

- Be at least 18 months of age,

- Be of good health and fitness levels

- Not be overweight or have joint issues

- Not be older than nine years (these dogs can compete but won't be eligible for prizes).

- Not be in heat (this is only applicable at the host club's discretion. Some allow dogs in heat to participate).

Most of Australia's agility competitions have their own requirements for dogs to enter. It depends primarily on your type of competition and category.

Breed Requirements

Again, much like the ACK, the ANKC allows all dog breeds to compete in agility competitions. Still, they might have to stick to specific categories. These can be based on experience levels ranging from novice to advanced. It can also include competitions based on breed size.

The Kennel Club (KC): United Kingdom

The Kennel Club is "the largest organization in the UK devoted to dog health, welfare, and training. [Their] objective is to ensure that dogs live healthy, happy lives with responsible owners" (The Kennel Club).

Agility Competition Regulations

It's a bit more complicated to group the agility regulations in the UK because different laws are applicable in different countries or nations. One prominent example is the docking of tails.

Eligibility Requirements

Suppose you want your dog to compete in agility competitions. In that case, it must first be eligible for different qualifying heats before moving on to the next level. Look at the KC's website to see their competition regulations and familiarize yourself beforehand. However, like the ACK, the Kennel Club has general eligibility requirements, which state that your dog must:

- Be 18 months or older to compete for prizes. However, if your dog is younger, you can enter the Not for Competition (NC) categories from four months of age.

- Be registered at the Kennel Club per Kennel Club Regulations for Classification and Registration.

- Not be aggressive or have a savage disposition.

- Not be in heat if it's a female.

- Not have an infectious disease.

If you are in the UK, look for the competitions you want to partake in and see whether your dog is eligible.

Breed Requirements

Again, most dog breeds can participate in agility competitions in the UK, but some are more strict than others. They don't specify which breeds are not allowed, depending on the type of competition you enter. For example, some competitions are for smaller breed dogs while others are for larger breeds. At the same time, some clubs might have Not for Competition events with their own breed specifications. To know whether your dog can compete, first look for the competition and its specific requirements.

Conclusion

Agility training can be a fun activity for dogs and owners. Still, it can also become a sport in which you can compete. But, although all dogs can do agility, some are more prone to figure out how it works quicker than others. Luckily, it doesn't matter which dog breed you have; if you are interested in this sport, you can start training your dog as soon as possible.

With these basic step-by-step instructions, you can have hours of fun with your fur friend while stimulating its body and mind. And the exciting part is that you don't have to go to a dog school to do it. You can buy or make the equipment and start your dog's training today. It's that easy.

Whether you want to compete or do it for fun, keep this guide handy to help navigate your training sessions with your dog. Once these basics are under wraps, you can consider going into more advanced practices. To top it all off, you can strengthen the bond you share in the process. You're on the right track; as long as you are patient, consistent, and provide positive reinforcement.

References

American Kennel Club. "American Kennel Club." American Kennel Club, 2017, www.akc.org/.

The Australian National Kennel Council. "Mission Statement." Ankc.org.au, ankc.org.au/AboutUs/?id=2403.

The Kennel Club. "About the Kennel Club - Partners, History and Memberships." www.thekennelclub.org.uk, www.thekennelclub.org.uk/about-us/about-the-kennel-club/.

Printed in Great Britain
by Amazon

22954083R00039